Heart *and* Sole

Heart *and* Sole

· ·

THE SHOES OF MY LIFE

WRITTEN AND ILLUSTRATED BY

Jane Eldershaw

St. Martin's Press

New York

www.stmartins.com

Book design by Michelle McMillian

Library of Congress Cataloging-in-Publication Data

Eldersaw, Jane.
   Heart and Sole: the shoes of my life/Jane Eldershaw.—1st ed.
     p. cm.
   ISBN 0-312-32304-2
   EAN 978-0312-32304-2
     1. Shoes—Social aspects. I. Title.
   GT2130.E43 2004
   391.4'13—dc22   2003070877

First Edition: May 2004

10   9   8   7   6   5   4   3   2   1

ACKNOWLEDGMENTS

I am deeply grateful to Nichole Argyres, Megan Buckley, Sheree Bykofsky, Karen Gillis, and Michelle McMillian for their professionalism, enthusiasm, and good ideas.

Some of my friends let me use parts of their shoe memories to enhance my own, or helped in other ways. With thanks, love, and gratitude to Alison Clark, Dee Anne Dyke, Audrey Farolino, Pauline Fingleton, Ann Marleen Hissink, Freddie Kaad, Gaynor Kaad, Cindy Kilian, Elisabeth MacIntyre, Deborah Moseley, Viki Sizgoric, Sandy Reingold, and Julie Walker.

And special thanks to George Ladas and the witty, urbane, and always elegant Susan Hurley from Inverell.

Give a girl the right shoes
and she can conquer the world.

—BETTE MIDLER

THE IMELDAS: GIRLFRIENDS
WHO LOVE SHOES

. . . .

Bonding via Shoes

There are only two kinds of women in the world. Those who love shoes and those who had the misfortune to be born without the ability to experience total bliss on finding a pair of perfectly designed pumps in the right size at half price. There's a direct correlation: the more shoes a woman owns, the nicer person she turns out to be. The more she obsesses about footwear, the more normal she becomes.

Those of us who love shoes are happy, passionate, exuberant people. Whenever we meet, we recognize each other with our own special greeting, the shoe-aholic's hello: "Ooooh," we say. "Cute *shoes.*"

I call them the Imeldas, the friends I go shoe-shopping

with, named in honor of the patron saint of footwear, Imelda Marcos, with her three-thousand-pair wardrobe.

Calling it simply *shopping*, though, is an understatement. Shopping implies an efficient task completed, a quick commercial transaction, a mere exchange of money for goods. What we do is a sort of moving meditation with stream-of-consciousness voice-over, a multitasking way of bonding. Quality time. We case our favorite stores, catch up on each other's news, sound out each other's opinions, and pursue our personal quest for the perfect comfort-to-style-ratio heel, all at the same time. We roam freely, pausing whenever a shoe catches our eye, exploring every delight each store has to offer. All our senses are satisfied: we finger taffeta slides, inhale the fragrance of new leather, test-drive four-inch stilettos, gossip outrageously.

It's not just shopping. It's also relaxing, stimulating, and productive—a hobby and a necessity and a pleasure all in one.

And it's practical to shop *à deux*. Step into a pair of lace-up reptile demi-boots, and you try on a whole new personality. But is it one you will be able to live with? Is this true lust or just fashion-victim myopia? An Imelda will tell you.

Or you fall in love with a pair of two-tone wingtips, but are not entirely sure it's a look you can pull off—a biased opinion is standing right next to you at the full-length mirror. There is empowerment in the buddy system. If you've lost all sense of perspective when it comes to open-toed wedges, an Imelda will help you just say no. And you can't beat an Imelda for a quick, efficient, all-purpose, on-the-spot rationalization: *You're actually saving money in the end. You'll wear them forever. They'll go with everything. You definitely need both pairs.*

You tap into years of vital shoe experience when you shop with an Imelda. (*I used to have a pair of mushroom-colored suede flats like this. Biggest mistake of my life. First time I wore them, they were ruined by fragrance-spray fallout.*) You learn that slides are not made for journeys of longer than two blocks, that navy-dyed pumps worn without hose can leave your toes looking bruised, that some stores will let you return virgin, unscuffed shoe mistakes.

Sometimes one of us is in the grip of a powerful urge to spend a lot of money we don't actually have. If my credit cards are maxed out (*Don't let me a buy a single thing today!*), looking at shoes is a way of cruising the malls without getting hurt. I can rely on an Imelda to talk me down from a fatal attraction.

Sometimes we are miserable, shoe-browsing to alleviate the pain of a broken heart, and mostly content to just walk and talk, but maybe making a few Prozac purchases—Kiwi polish, shoe trees—to get back into the swing of things.

Sometimes we go to discount stores, poverty-stricken spendthrifts, and acquire multiple pairs of brightly colored plastic sandals. Buying too much too cheaply—it's the shopper equivalent of overdosing on sugar. We spend money, we get silly and excitable—it's more cathartic than chocolate.

Sometimes there are three of us. We move through department stores, a tangle of girls all talking at once, drawn by anything bright and colorful. We gravitate to Designer Shoes, reaffirming our taste for ultra-skinny straps, squealing over red satin lining, plucking a pump from its pedestal, turning it over to check its pedigree, making our way, guided by some infallible inner radar, to the sales racks, instantly on heightened alert for our own particular size.

All morning we claim we don't need rest, food, or water, just shoes, until we all get ravenous at the same time and tell ourselves that lunch will give us a chance to decide about the thigh-high pink python boots, whether they're a have-to-have we can't live without—or whether, come to think of it, what we really, truly *need* are the leopard-skin elf booties.

> Shoes are not mere accessories.
> Shoes are the meaning of life.

Shoes, we agree, are the most satisfactory way to spend money: more gratifyingly public than lingerie, bigger and more show-offy than jewelry, friendlier, and cozier than the cold metal of technology.

Shoes are not mere accessories. Shoes are the meaning of life.

DÉJÀ SHOE ALL OVER AGAIN

. . . .

First Steps for Little Folk

There once existed a shaky eight-millimeter home movie, crackling with static, of me staggering about in my first shoes, out in the backyard of our suburban bungalow.

The voice-over is Dad: "Hold it *steady*, Betty, damn it," he says as the garden lurches toward the camera and then tilts to show him—still dark-haired, boyish even—making frantic hand motions: "No, no . . . Stop that! Not me. Goddamn it, Betty, turn the thing off, you're wasting film." But Mom swings back to zoom in on Baby Jane, alone on a vast stretch of lawn, yet to master the art of walking in a straight line.

I look down at my own feet, entranced . . . so busy focusing on my new, white, calf T-straps that I almost fall over. They have tiny ventilation holes in decorative patterns, and my feet are so small that the shoes are almost round—snub-nosed and chubby, cute as a teddy bear.

And, in fact, when we were tiny tots, shoes *were* like toys, toys that adults put on our feet. My favorite were a pair of bunny slippers: little pink, woolen sockettes with embroidered noses and white ears and buttons for eyes—hand-knitted, haute couture courtesy of Grandmama. And galoshes made satisfying loud thumps clumping through the house. *(Hear that? It's me! I can make noise! I exist!)* Ballet slippers (plus a tiara and a pink net tutu and fairy wings covered in sparkly rhinestones) were a perfectly splendid choice for a trip to the supermarket.

And if shoes were toys, buying new ones was a fine game. Remember stepping onto those measuring things, feeling the cold metal through your socks, the slider defining the limits of your footprint on the world? The clerk would return with a whole armload of possibilities—gift boxes! She and your mother were wholly focused on you, asking what you liked, which you wanted, were they comfy? Competent fingers buttoned mary janes, adjusted buckles, pulled shoelaces snug. The saleslady's thumb would press down to feel how much space there was between your toe and the end of the shoe as she made little whispered asides to your mother: "Room to grow . . . very popular this season . . . reliable brand name.

Queen for a day, Cinderella, a princess with servants

Walk 'round, sweetheart. How do they feel?" Your comfort was anxiously attended to, you were queen for a day, Cinderella, a princess with servants.

Everything is fine until we start caring what other people think.

That's when the Dark Ages in my life as a shoe diva began. It was not until my teens that footwear became something to love, honor, and accumulate. Between the ages of six and twelve, I was a hidebound traditionalist, desperate to fit in at school and fanatical about looking exactly like everyone else.

Once, halfway to grade school, I realized, with horror, that I still had bedroom slippers on, rather than the regulation oxford brogues that were part of a strictly enforced school uniform. Not properly dressed! For the first time, clothing caused sharp embarrassment, and shoes let me down. I became fallible, human, unsure. Outfit anxiety! It was the beginning of growing insecurities, the end of innocence.

The carefree part of my childhood was over. Adults were trying to fill the large empty spaces in my brain—the spaces that would later be filled with images of shoe styles—with things like mental arithmetic. And it was about this time that my grade school teacher took to announcing our daily song to the class by saying: *Now we will all sing and Jane will hum.*

Between the ages of six and twelve, I was desperate to fit in at school and fanatical about looking exactly like everyone else.

I'd been a happy only child. Now the world was suddenly overrun with teasing schoolmates and demanding teachers. I tried to gain control over the few things I could: I insisted on footwear identical to that of everyone else, insisted that replacement pairs look exactly the same as those I'd worn previously.

During those lost years, the main part of my shoe wardrobe contained only two kinds of shoes: one pair of brown lace-up brogues, for school, and one pair of Good Shoes, black patent leather flats that we called court shoes, for parties and outings. The court shoes had a flattened grosgrain bow glued on the instep, and I always wore them with white cotton socks neatly folded over at the ankle, just the way everyone else did.

Luckily these lean years did not scar me for life. I am proud to say that I was able to triumph over the fear of exerting my individuality and later developed a keen appreciation for a beautifully sculpted heel, an abiding love of exotic leathers, and an eagle eye for a pump that is both flattering and unusual. In fact, some friends speculate that the tragic ugly-school-shoe trauma was perhaps the defining experience of my childhood, that it actually led me to become the adroit shoe shopper, the dedicated collector, and the single-minded footwear fanatic I am today.

But I prefer to think that my driving motivation comes from those early happy memories of tottering along on the lawn, that original delight in shoes as playthings. Whenever I see very young children trying on new footwear, a three-year-old, say, on an adult-size chair with feet sticking straight out, waggling his ankles, admiring his new T-straps or jellies or sneakers, I replay in my mind the unsteady baby footsteps of wonder captured in that home movie, and I remember new-shoe joy all over again.

MY FAMILY SHOE TREE: A TALE
OF TWO CLOSETS

· ·

Fitting In vs. Standing Out

Fifty-six pairs, all in their original boxes—that was my mother's personal best. Each box labeled with black laundry marker: large, careful capitals spelling out OXFORDS, *black and white*; OXFORDS, *navy and white*; OXFORDS, *tan and white*, a lifetime's supply of shoes carefully laid down in their own closet like fine wine. My father said shoes were her way of making up for being a middle child.

But it was more than that. Footwear was Mother's chosen method of representing Quality. Good Shoes demonstrated, even more reliably than pearls or twinsets, essential attributes such as Quiet Elegance and Refined Breeding. Good Shoes showed, in a genteel, understated way, that you Knew What Was What. When my mother talked about shoes, she used

My Mother's Tips for Caring for Good Shoes

- Get shoe trees for good shoes that you wear a lot. Pairs that you rarely wear will be okay with tissue—or keep the cardboard shapes that came inside the shoes when you bought them.
- Fine leather needs to be polished regularly. Ask a man with beautifully maintained brogues which shoe-shine guy he uses. And you don't have to be in your shoes when they are shined—take them with their trees inside.
- Even when you're in love with a pair, it's not a good idea to live in them. Leather is porous and needs time to air out between wearings, so don't wear the same shoes two days in a row.
- Shoes that are in tones slightly darker than skin tone give the illusion of long legs, height, and elegance.

phrases like *impeccable style*, *quality leather*, and *classic lines*—as if the sleek thoroughbreds she wore on her feet (Ferragamo, Delman, Bally) had pedigrees and heritage and provenance, as if they strode through a world of antiques, racehorses, and ancient lineage, rather than one of PTA meetings, supermarket checkout lines, and chauffeuring the kids.

The Ferragamo-appreciation gene had been passed on to her from my grandmother, who smelled of clean cotton handkerchiefs and Coty face powder and, when I was very young, instructed me never to tell a man that my feet hurt. "It sounds so

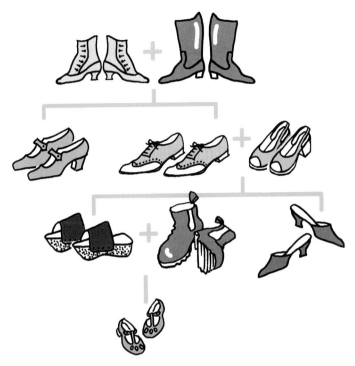

vulgar," she told me. "Instead, say, 'My foot hurts.' Much classier."

The flip side of my shoe education was Aunt Doris. If my mother's shoes were her personal walking advertisement of refinement, my father's sister (from the "my feet hurt" side of the family) considered shoes a badge of freedom. She'd grown up during the Depression, when even the ugliest, most utilitarian new shoes were an outrageous indulgence. As a teenager,

My Aunt's Tips for Caring for Good Shoes

- Shoes that are made of synthetic materials trap the sweat from your feet and end up smelling nasty, especially if you don't wear hose. So sprinkle deodorant foot powder inside new shoes. Ideally, any shoes you buy made of plastic should be open, like sandals.
- Plastic soles can be extremely slippery. Take a cab.
- Of course you're not going to let the possibility of hammertoes, corns, bunions, and back pain keep you from the pleasure of walking into a party in a pair of pointy-toed peau de soie evening shoes dotted with rhinestones. But please remember to vary your heel height most days and do calf-stretching exercises religiously to avoid ending up with feet permanently arched, like Barbie.
- Shoes are the only part of your outfit that you can get a perfect view of any time you want. So whatever you decide to put on your feet, be sure it puts a smile on your face whenever you look down.

she'd had to endure chunky, practical wartime clodhoppers: sturdy brown lace-up brogues and hand-me-down winter boots. As soon as she could afford it, her footwear philosophy became, *The sexier, the better.*

My mother owned sensible loafers, genteel spectators, and demure flats. My aunt owned ankle-strap toe-peeper wedgies, high-heeled marabou scuffs, and snakeskin spikes.

Mom's shoes had smooth, dull textures and colors like tan, taupe, cordovan, navy, and luggage. Aunt Doris had good-time girl stilettos covered in Thai silk dyed a glorious shade of Schiaparelli pink, red high-heeled slingbacks with gold heels, fabric-covered platforms in loud flower prints.

My mother's shoes whispered quiet good taste; my aunt's shoes shouted "Wheee!"

Guess which closet was most fun to burrow through? Aunt Doris let me play dress-up in her wardrobe, and I became an instant princess in gold mules or pink satin slides. At Aunt Doris's place I didn't drag out coloring pencils or picture books; instead I'd find a pair of her four-inch dyed-blue ostrich spikes, climb aboard, and totter in to where the adults were to hear the shoes' story.

My aunt would smile when she saw what I had on. "Those are my favorites."

"My God," my mother would say. "Stilettos! I can't walk in them. They say Marilyn Monroe always has one heel of her stilettos cut shorter than the other, so she'll walk sexy. I don't believe it. It's hard enough to walk in them anyway."

Aunt Doris nodded. "Street gratings. My heels always get caught. And they ruin everything . . . carpets, linoleum—Jack won't let me near the parquet. But gee, aren't they gorgeous?"

Even more luxurious, it seemed to me in those early Barbie doll days, was Aunt Doris's enduring edict that shoes must always go with your handbag.

"Everything matchy-matchy—that's my rule. I've owned some real neat outfits in my time," she told me. "I used to have the smartest shantung sheath—Lord & Taylor—that went with those blue stilettos. And a matching pillbox hat. And gloves, blue suede."

Both women had about the same number of shoes, but my aunt's purchases spanned a longer time period. Aunt Doris kept shoes she hadn't worn for thirty years—no way would she ever throw out her favorites, mementos of good times that stretched back for decades. She still had the candy-colored cocktail-party mules and the cork-soled poolside-barbecue sandals she wore through the fifties, the beaded ballerinas she danced the Twist in during the sixties, the sexy platforms that took her disco-ing in the seventies. Every size six was a souvenir of life lived to the fullest.

My mother, meanwhile, discarded shoes the moment they looked the

> At Aunt Doris's I'd find a pair of her four-inch dyed-blue ostrich spikes and climb aboard.

slightest bit crestfallen and replaced them with yet more trust-worthy, long-distance-performing, almond-toe, chunky, mid-heel pumps.

My closet reflects those dual shoe roots. Half of me is a quiet, shy good girl; the other half is a demonstrative show-off. Half of me has classic, conservative good taste; the other half loves funny, outrageous, eye-catching styles. Half my shoe purchases are enduring perennials; the other half are one-summer wonders, footwear fads, and flash. I waver between wanting to fit in and trying to stand out. Between frumpy and fabulous, dowdy and divine.

Most days I follow in my mom's footsteps. The usual me wears demure pumps in real leather with medium heels. But when I want to do hard-core glamour, I know which relative inspires me.

FINDING A SHOE-INN FOR STORAGE

Everywhere but in the Closet

I still have the same point-of-use shoe storage system I had at age five. This is not progress.

When I was little, each type of shoe lived in a different habitat. Flip-flops lived near the beach towels at the bottom of the linen closet. Bunny slippers shared space under the bed with the dust bunnies. Galoshes were supposed to live in the big wooden box near the laundry, but usually landed with a rubbery thump under the hooks laden with plastic raincoats in the hall.

I still store shoes in a variety of different places. But now it's the *What was I thinking?* purchases that languish under the bed: gruesome gladiator sandals, never-worn high-heeled sneakers, walking shoes that are way too pedestrian.

Here lie unfortunate mistakes like the strappy, green, disco-queen baby heels that are gorgeous and sexy and go with nothing at all. Here are the flip-flops that chafe between the big and second toe, the toe-scrunching metallic mules, the slip-ons that turned out to be slip-ups, and all the other missteps along the path to true shoe happiness.

My current favorite shoes are enthroned on built-in racks at the front of the closet—only twelve pairs allowed for. At the back is a Bermuda Triangle of tangled straps and interlocked heels, containing old reliables like the gold slides that have been repaired every summer for three years. (Strangers still ask me where I got them.)

Bunny slippers shared space under the bed with the dust bunnies.

The sandals that got caught in a rainstorm are drying out in the bathroom. The champagne-stained fabric-covered party pumps are undergoing substance-abuse rehabilitation therapy at the shoe repair shop. New shoes—the half-price alligator pumps, the stilettos I bought in the midst of a delirious heel high—are housed in a leaning tower of shoe boxes, waiting for their first outing. The plain black pumps I wear every day lie scattered apart and pigeon-toed across the wall-to-wall.

Should the living quarters of a grown woman look like this?

I consider introducing order into my life. I pore over advertisements for companies that promise to reduce chaos painlessly, to engineer your closet to hold your entire wardrobe neatly, every item visible and at hand. It's a seductive idea. You can't help feeling that if you had the perfect closet, everything else would fall into place. The rest of life would be perfect, too.

I need a second opinion. I call a well-shod friend, a fellow footwear fanatic, to talk shoe-storage strategy. I ask how many pairs she has. Gazillions. Yes, but just how many is that?

"Wayyyyy too many. Hold on one second. . . ." I hear her *clip-clop* over to her closet. "Ten, twelve, fifteen . . ." A little gasp. "Fifty-two. I didn't think I had that many. And that's not counting sneakers and flip-flops and stuff in Manhattan Mini Storage. And, I still really, really, desperately need a pair of gold kid evening heels."

"But where will you put them?"

"Shoes are too cool to put away! I like looking at them, lined up like little soldiers. Even if I never wear them, I know they're there, emitting style molecules into the air."

This is a gratifying revelation: another shoe diva as impractical as I am about storage. I ask her about the closet cleaner-upperers, the systems mavens who group and index and apportion shoe-rack real estate.

"For God's sake, don't do it! If you think your shoe storage problems are bad now, they'll be twice as bad when they're solved. You haven't thought this through. Those systems 'fix' your closet to hold just twenty pairs. It would mean never being able to buy another pair without first tossing an old pair. No room for serendipity, no latitude for earth-shatteringly momentous sales or lucky shopportunities . . ."

Months later, my shoes are still scattered throughout the apartment, plus they have taken over the kitchen. On the countertop are taffeta slipper slingbacks having their inner-soles glued back down, red suede ankle boots recuperating after being sprayed with water repellent, and the two-tone spectators that take hours to clean because the white polish gets on the blue toe and the navy polish ruins the white parts, and, no matter how careful you are, all those little perforations clog up with gunk.

Do I want to live like this? Shouldn't I be over this manic desire to pursue superficial passions? And do I really, truly need more than twenty pairs of shoes?

Of course I do.

THE FENG-SHOE-Y
OF BRIDESMAID FOOTWEAR

Fantasy Shoes

I attribute my life-long quest for beautiful shoes to two defining events that occurred at an impressionable age. The first was being shipped off to the local School of Deportment for a major overhaul; the second was serving time as a bridesmaid.

I was twelve—the perfect age to be a bridesmaid. In fact, my friends and I spent a lot of time that year planning our own weddings. It was the next step after wanting a horse. We deliberated for hours over gowns, color schemes, china patterns, and flatware designs. We had our guest lists all drawn up and the entire bridal ceremony carefully choreographed— all without the annoyance of having to consider the wishes of anyone else, especially the young men who would be our partners for life.

I did not, however, have any say in my bridesmaid's gown for the actual wedding I was to take part in. I was not present for the many conferences concerning ivory taffeta and snowflake lace edging and Sabrina necklines and butterfly sleeves and cathedral length trains and petal-shaped veils. I was simply taken to a dressmaker to be fitted for a gold satin Empire-line dress with matching pointy-toed pumps.

My mother felt that a little more fairy-godmothering was needed—she wasn't sure that head-to-toe gold satin alone would work enough Cinderella-type magic. The emergency course at the School of Deportment was her desperate attempt to improve my posture and give me at least a thin veneer of poise before the big day.

However, instead of providing encouragement and instilling confidence, the Charm Police who scrutinized me at the school pointed out problems that I had been unaware, up to now, I had: shapeless legs plus arches that tend to lean inward. These revelations made me so miserable, I wanted to forget the whole thing.

Then the finished bridesmaid ensemble arrived. In it, I felt like a princess: the style of the dress was unexpectedly flattering, the shoes even more so. The one-inch stacked heel helped me walk in a less flat-footed manner than usual, and the extreme pointiness of the toes seemed to lengthen my legs—

The style of the dress was unexpectedly flattering, the shoes even more so.

or at least divert attention away from them. This was far, far better than dress-up: I'd be able to assume this disguise again whenever I wanted. And not only did I feel like a princess, but I was actually treated like one, as well, a distinct improvement on real life. Everyone oohed and aahed and told me I looked absolutely adorable and a lot of satisfactory fuss was made. The Charm School made me aware that I wasn't beautiful, but the wedding made me aware that shoes could help fake it.

I became hooked on the transforming power and possibilities of flattering shoes; conscious for the first time that they are a new identity, a rejuvenation, an instant makeover. Slip on a pair of elegant, high-quality pumps, and they instantly transfer that elegance and quality over to you. (The pavement-protecting properties are a bonus.) Shoes are a transformation you can make quickly and while sitting down. Forget exercycles, liposuction, or professionally shaped eyebrows. Shoes are much faster and more effective than any of these.

At age twelve, the strangest part of the wedding for me was the bride's tears during the ceremony. I was positioned behind her, incredulous. She was so overcome by emotion that her shoulders began to heave convulsively at the altar and she started weeping. I couldn't understand it. What on earth was there to cry about? This was the happiest day of her life. She was wearing to-die-for hand-embroidered shoes sewn with tiny seed pearls.

I am by no means an expert. (That was my first and last appearance on stage, as it were, at a wedding.) I do, however, have opinions about some of the frequently anguished shoe dilemmas facing bridesmaids.

For example, I advocate one-night-stand footwear. Most people look for good quality shoes they can wear again. But why bother? It's entirely possible you'll find a wonderful pair of cute kitten heels or bracelet-strap sandals that go well with the dress but don't cost a fortune. If the reception is any fun at all, the shoes will be ruined by champagne as you dance an abandoned Lambada with the groom's grandfather. A wedding is a wonderful excuse to ignore practicality.

So try to persuade the bride to let you go your own way with shoes. Insisting that everyone and everything match means that the six of you will look, in photos, like a bad girl's group from the fifties.

Then, look for shoes in regular shoe stores, not just bridal salons. Think festive. Approach this as a chance to live out your own Cinderella fantasies, to buy the kind of girlish and glittery dress-up shoes you might not normally wear, with features like diamanté buckles, gold mesh, and sparkly heels. Above all, find a pair of shoes that has that magical transforming power.

Because when you feel like a princess, you become one.

TRAINING HEELS

. . . .

My First Unrequited Love

I was thirteen, a teenager. I was on the threshold of everything wonderful—or would be, I was sure, if only I were allowed to step over that threshold in heels and lipstick.

My mother and I were locked in a full-scale battle of wills. Inexplicably, she refused to see that heels would transform me from child to femme fatale, that self-confidence, poise, and allure could be easily purchased.

"Those little spikes are unstable," said my mother, impervious to fashion, "and common," her all-purpose, utility word of dismissal. She retained her lifelong fondness for (*eeuch!*) lady-like, low, square, stacked heels.

Muth-errrr! Sensible, stacked heel wearers always made

WHAT IS THAT HEEL CALLED

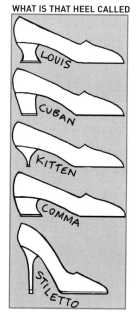

LOUIS

CUBAN

KITTEN

COMMA

STILETTO

their beds, shushed people in movie theaters, and had no interest in boys.

But arguments and guerrilla warfare were to no avail. We maintained a facade of armed neutrality until I remembered that tried-and-true childhood tactic: The best way to get a gerbil is to start out by asking for a pony. I told Mom I was saving up for teetering three-inch stilettos.

It wasn't true. Instinctively, I knew I wasn't ready for *high* high heels. I had no idea what the "courtship strut" was, or that heels gave it to you by forcing your body into a posture that emphasizes your breasts and behind. I wasn't aware that the tensed ankle plus extended leg is the biological sign of sexual availability in most animal species. All I knew was that height was tricky, that walking in high heels was obviously an adult attribute, like being able to eat oysters without gagging.

What I yearned for was exactly what the fashion magazines mandated: a low, junior version of the stiletto—kitten heels. But we didn't call them that, then. To us they were Little Heels, curvy and cute.

And I wanted my heels to be curvy and cute, even if I wasn't.

Convincing my mother was easier than expected.

All the forces of youth and marketing were with me. Every single model in *Seventeen* and *Mademoiselle* wore long, slender Little Heels, and department stores featured them in a big way in advertisements with elongated sketches of glorious sleek pumps with impossibly long, narrow, pointed toes. The message was clear: Little Heels were cool. I couldn't take my rightful place as a teenager without them.

The spirit of Hubris, picking its teeth in the shadows, lies in wait for young girls with longings such as these.

Every weekend my mother and I would choose a different area of combat. We'd start the day with hope, and only intermittent small-arms fire. Mom would drag me through the big department store in town, showing me the chaste, dowdy, boring shoes she'd be happy to buy me. Ugly, uglier,

I was wearing the objects of my deepest desire, and they were stunning—I was the one who was lacking.

ugliest. I'd pull her toward our little neighborhood boutiques, looking for a spark of magic among the tame, the durable, the practical, the useful. Then we'd hit the malls and begin all over again, as hostilities escalated.

Until, finally, there they were, in the most unlikely store, waiting for me, side by side, elevated to their rightful place on a display pedestal with a spotlight shining on them, a light from heaven. And—the ultimate good omen!—the pair sitting there was my size. I'd found the perfect kittens, I was in love.

Convincing my mother was easier than expected. She was tired, her feet were aching, she was more than ready to capitulate. I promised to wear the shoes everywhere, with everything, forever. My mother surrendered. Maybe the heel was a bit narrow, but they were bone, a ladylike, all-purpose color she approved of. We both wanted to call it a day and go home victorious.

Trying them on was a mere formality. They were mine. I was euphoric, until I tried to walk and wobbled at each step. I looked at myself in the mirror, transfixed in horror. Even standing still, with one shoulder forward, hand on hip, feet at a ten-to-two angle, in classic runway pose, the shoes did nothing to disguise what were—let's face it—flat feet and piano legs. *Full-grown* flat feet on a half-grown body. This time the transformation process hadn't worked. I was wearing the objects of my deepest desire, and they were stunning—I was the one who was lacking. I needed new legs to live up to my shoes. Or, preferably, a whole new body.

When people said, *Beware of getting what you want*, this is what they meant. I'd won the battle with my mother but lost the war. And the spirit of Hubris was chuckling loudly, in the knowledge that a lifetime of searching for flattering shoes lay ahead.

WHITE GO-GO BOOTS, DARK NIGHTS

Preparing for the Worst

For most people, dressing for parties is routine preparation—they get ready, then go out and have a fabulous time. I actually prefer the dressing-up part, when I have a legitimate excuse to try on every single pair of heels in my wardrobe. For me, *that's* the fabulous time.

These days, I don't bother trying to present perfection to the world. As a teenager, it seemed essential, given the many tragic deficiencies I'd been born with. In order to look the least bit normal, I had to put in contacts instead of wear glasses, add a Dynel fall of false hair, stuff tissues in my bra, and line my eyes all around with black for the panda bear effect that looked so appealing on the magazine models of the time. It seemed necessary not so much to make up my face as to make up my *myself*.

These marathon grooming sessions started with one of the first unchaperoned parties I was allowed to go to alone, at age fifteen. It was a costume party, and I spent hours painstakingly dressing for success—the success I had in mind was with the opposite sex.

I had cunningly contrived a costume-party outfit that would highlight my proudest wardrobe acquisitions: I'd be a Wicked Witch, but a beautiful, hip, sleek one, naturally, in a wickedly alluring new black minidress. The homemade pointed hat I would whip off after the first introductions.

And the pièce de résistance would be my boots.

The mid-sixties was the golden age of boots. Jane Fonda wore wonderful boots, and so did Nancy Sinatra and Diana Rigg as Emma Peel in *The Avengers*. As miniskirts crept up, boots became taller. It was the golden age of vinyl, too—*the wet look*. (We actually used terms like that, then—as well as *kinky* and *mod* and *fab*—and we were straight-faced and serious when we used them.)

Boots would make me Catwoman-powerful at the party and cover less-than-spectacular legs. And what boots I had! They stood for everything that mattered to me then: innovative design, foreign flair, ostentatious luxury. They were flat-heeled, knee-high white patent leather with cutaway panels by André Courrèges—well, a copy, not the real thing, but even so, I can't begin to tell you how new and desirable go-go boots were at the time, and how I cherished my pair, acquired laboriously on the layaway system, painstakingly paid off over many months,

. . . .
The boots, of course, were a
consolation, but a private one.
. . . .

out of wages from my Saturday job behind the candy counter at the local cinema, mishandling ice cream.

These boots were everything one could ever ask for in footwear: they would make me look sensational, they would demonstrate immediately that I was on the cutting-edge of fashion, and they would inspire the envy of all.

My preparations for the party took on epic proportions.

Witch hazel and toothpaste, the current popular pimple-blasters, covered the acne, then came chalky foundation. Several hours with tweezers, individual false eyelashes, a fiddly little tube of glue, and a magnifying mirror gave me clumps of extra Twiggy-type eyelashes that sprang to attention in the most unnatural way. (I used two packets, on the principle that a thing that's worth doing is worth doing twice.)

Instead of lipstick I used Erace, a foundation stick that was designed to hide blemishes. This was another popular makeup trick of the mid-sixties: the hippest girls had no mouths at all.

There was a backup plan in place to smuggle Erace and eyeliner into the car and apply it on the way to the party in case my mother didn't allow me out of the house with raccoon eyes and totally obliterated lips, but luckily she thought this was all part of the witch disguise. (She seemed strangely blind to the fact that I had metamorphosed into a stunning and alluring teenage siren.)

Naturally, a gathering I'd placed such importance on was doomed. No gasps of incredulous delight were forthcoming on my arrival. None of the guys seemed capable of perceiving the great charm of my boots. The mass adulation I was expecting did not eventuate. The eligible males chose fetching blond bunny rabbits and soft, fuzzy bumblebees to pair up with in dark corners.

I won't dwell on the excruciating humiliation of that night except to report that, inevitably, I spent the evening standing around trying to look as if—had I wanted to—I could be engaging in sparkling repartee with anyone I chose. It was just that, right now, I was too fascinated by the books in the bookshelf to do anything else but simply stand there. The boots, of course, were a consolation, but a private one.

I went home. I took the tissues out of my bra. Five hours earlier I had never considered that there would be life after the party. Or, come to think of it, that there would ever be a time when I was not inordinately pleased with the snappy white shininess of those boots. (Now white footwear seems as unexciting as tennis skirts, bridal gowns, and laboratory overalls.)

I had been so sure the boots were going to do it all for me: demonstrate my innate sense of style and the fabulous life I was destined to lead. I was hoping that they would carry me along in the wake of their wonderfulness, that they would wear me, rather than the other way around. That they would tell the world that I was the sort of person who was at home in French designer boots—even though that night they felt as much fancy dress as the witch hat, as fake as the false eyelashes. No doubt, to everyone else at the party that night, the boots delivered a completely different message.

I still spend hours getting ready for parties, trying on all my shoes. But now I do it to please myself.

SEX AND THE SHOE

· ·

What Makes Footwear Alluring?

At seventeen, I found the whole sex thing very confusing. Especially how to look sexy. It took me years, for example, to grasp the concept that wearing shoes could be a sexier look than bare feet.

I drove my first, much-loved automobile barefoot. It was only a squat, preowned rust bucket, but it was my very own rust bucket, and it symbolized maturity and freedom. I can still taste that scary freedom as I drove home through the neon-washed downtown at night, alone in my small, square cocoon, wicked but safe, ready for adventure, fearful I'd find it. Kicking off shoes was part of the freedom. I'd read that Francoise Sagan, teenage author of *Bonjour Tristesse*, drove barefoot. It sounded so French, so wanton and abandoned. I

Shoes That Make Your Legs Look Great

The aim is to get the look of a long, slim leg and foot, and it's all done by optical illusion.

For example, by wearing pants, or hosiery the same color as your shoes, you create a long, unbroken line. Anything that distracts the eye when it travels down the body—shiny surfaces, bows, buckles, a change of color—will make your legs seem shorter.

This can also work the other way. On your feet, the abrupt change of a Chanel contrasting-colored cap-toe makes the foot look smaller.

- A low-cut pump with no straps lengthens the foot, so wear shoes with ankle straps only if you have long legs. If you love ankle strap shoes and have short legs, go for very fine, thin, skin-colored straps.
- Heavy, chunky heeled shoes will make your legs look heavy and chunky, too, unless you have very skinny legs, in which case they'll look even skinnier. Slimmer heels are slimming.
- Stilettos make the calves more shapely because when the heel is raised, the calf muscle becomes shortened and more prominent. You can get this look naturally by exercising: rise slowly up and down on your toes whenever you are standing around.
- When you do wear stilettos, be aware of your posture—high heels make some women hunch forward unattractively.
- Shoes with even a little heel—one inch, for example—are more flattering than totally flat shoes, especially with pants.
- The higher the shoe, the wider the pants you can wear with it; the flatter the shoe, the narrower the pants can be. No-heel shoes give no support to your arches and make your feet look flat if you don't have high arches.
- If boots cut off at the widest part of your calf, they will draw attention to it—a good look for skinny legs, not so good for thick legs.
- Pointed-toe shoes give more of an illusion of height than round toes do.

had to do it, too. I was a certified bohemian, now—an art student. Driving barefoot seemed like the least I could do.

As art students, we studied nakedness. Every week, in Life Class, there was a new model, mostly female but sometimes male, for us to attempt to represent in two dimensions. We tried to concentrate on the lumpy, unairbrushed, unsupported flesh in front of us (bright pink on the side that was nearest the space heater, mottled blue on the far side) in a way that showed we were serious artists concerned with planes and shadows and proportion, anatomy and the laws of perspective, and not wide-eyed, dirty-minded kids. It took some of us a good ten minutes of careful, concentrated pencil-sharpening before we could face unadorned, ugly reality.

When the novelty of nudism wore off after a few months, I realized that most bodies actually look better covered. I also realized that the molded-rubber, drugstore, garden-variety flip-flops that I wore when I wasn't barefoot, and which I imagined made me look sexy, in a free-spirited, wild-child, hippie-waifish kind of way, didn't. I became aware that grubby feet (even seventeen-year-old feet, feet at the peak of their cuteness) flapping and flopping, slipping and slopping, did not catch a guy's attention the way high heels did.

"Which is sexier," I asked my first boyfriend, "bare feet or high heels?"

I realized that most bodies actually look better covered.

"They almost always wear high heels in the pictures in *Playboy* . . . ," he said.

I asked him how he knew that. (I was not only confused, but also very naive.)

So I, too, turned to magazines for enlightenment. Fashion magazines.

That summer my favorite magazine showed strappy sandals that seemed incredibly sexy. I coveted a pair whose main means of support were wraparound ribbon laces that made legs look as if they were gift-wrapped. The copy printed next to the picture mentioned the eroticism of corsets, the excitement of unlacing, even the visual subtext of bondage and dominatrix weirdness. Here was a truly sexy shoe. I decided to follow the magazine's advice to invest (that was their word, *invest*) in the strappy, lace-up sandals. Then I spent hours experimenting with those laces. The fashion-page pictures—carefully composed, art directed, *static* pictures—showed how the straps could be tied in many different ways: they could extend to the top of the calves, or be wrapped many times around the ankle and fastened with a bow. You could start by taking the ribbons around the back, then climb them upward, or you could crisscross the instep first, and then take them behind to secure the heel. What the magazine didn't mention was that no matter how you tied them, the ribbons loosened up and slid under your foot after just five minutes of walking, forcing you to stutter-step along clumsily until you could stop and adjust them. At which point you would look down to see a little toe sticking out at an odd angle, worming its way out of the side of the multiplicity of straps at the front of the shoe. Then you'd get a very unsexy look on your face when you remembered just how much you'd paid—*invested*—to look this way.

I realized too late that this was the same publication that had urged me to acquire the skyscraper stilettos that made me mince about like a giraffe and tower over most dates. Plus they'd all but guaranteed that slutty gold-sequined platforms would turn my nonexistent social life into one long sequin of events.

These were just a few of the early failures during the decades of research into trying to look sexy. I don't think I ever managed to buy my way to sensuous feet but I did learn one thing along the way: It's been my experience that there's no use in even worrying about looking sexy, because there's not really a lot you can do about it. You can buy fierce footwear yet end up looking foolish in it—the eye-appeal of five-inch stilettos is cancelled out when they're worn by someone lacking in heel skills. Some women look irresistible trying to scrape gum off their shoe, or painting their toenails, or lumbering around in snow boots. Everyday sneakers are just as likely to put the

Toe décolletage

moon and the stars in optimal alignment as strappy sandals. Some guys find boots a turn-on, others don't.

Maybe the sexiest shoes are very subtly sexy, like those with toe décolletage—that hint of cleavage revealed when shoes are cut low enough in front to expose the split between the big toe and the next toe. Confidence probably has a lot to do with sexiness. And love. (Loving the shoes you're wearing, that is.) When you find shoes that manage to make you feel sexy, like flat turquoise sandals that are delicate enough to evoke heavenly holidays and summer happiness and transform you, when you wear them, into Audrey Hepburn in the south of France—buy them immediately. You'll feel incredibly sexy every time you put them on, and that, in the end, is the important thing.

PLATFORMS: THE MUSICAL

The Height of Absurdity, the Sound of Individuality

Let me tell you about my platform shoes. They were wood . . . and not some tacky look-of-woodgrain synthetic camouflaging a lightweight cork sole, either. No way. I clumped my way through the seventies, a pioneer of elevated footwear and violently colored tie-dyed T-shirts and proud of it. Ask any veteran of that era what it was like to haul bricks with each step—when they've finished hooting about the hairstyles, they'll tell you. Call those things you see in the shops today platforms? *Phuh!* They're just pale, watered-down imitations. The original platforms were cement shoes that moored you to the ground like an inflatable, rebounding punching toy. One false move on those babies, and you woke up in traction.

My platforms were two hunks of timber that could have

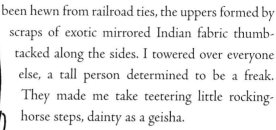

been hewn from railroad ties, the uppers formed by scraps of exotic mirrored Indian fabric thumb-tacked along the sides. I towered over everyone else, a tall person determined to be a freak. They made me take teetering little rocking-horse steps, dainty as a geisha.

Five inches high (I measured) and heavy and inflexible and probably the cause of my current chronic pronating arches, flat feet, and weak ankles. Gosh, they were wonderful.

Platforms are look-at-me shoes, and that's what I wanted then—adolescent fame, a by-product of look-at-me-I'm-an-individual posturing. For several years platforms were my self-confidence, my Look, my only footwear.

It wasn't just me; it was the seventies. (I take comfort in that.) It's the fate of teenagers to embarrass themselves in the process of finding out who they are through what they wear. Our generation simply chose to do it more flam-

The original platforms were cement shoes that moored you to the ground like an inflatable, rebounding punching toy.

boyantly than most, in a style of shoe that is downright ugly and flatters no one—an accident waiting to happen.

Parents hated them—a large part of their allure. I imagined I was a rebel, yet I wore platforms like everyone else, chunky, exuberant, the size of tugboats. Mine were actually pretty tame for the time. People were clonking along on clear plastic soles so big, aquatic creatures could, and did, swim in them; pounding out a pavement drumbeat in Dr. Scholl's; clattering around in shoes seven to eight inches high, covered in rhinestones and sequins or swirly, bright psychedelic colors. Platform shoes were a memorable, discordant instance of collective self-delusion: our generation's reaction to the middle-class, suburban fifties, when the ultimate sin was to stand out.

Yes, big shoes are attention getting—the same way spinach on your teeth is attention getting.

The closest I've come to being famous was courtesy of those shoes: I wore them continually at college, and everyone knew I was around by the staccato of my big clumpies. For some reason I felt it necessary to seek out the most ungainly examples of the genre, to have the biggest and noisiest on campus. My huge wooden platforms clip-clopping along a street caused pedestrians ahead of me on the sidewalk to look back in alarm, expecting to see, at the very least, that they were being pursued by an officer mounted on horseback.

As I reminisce, I'm trying to justify this lunacy. I'd like to be able to say that my platforms were my own personal performance-art piece, that my shoes were beating out a tattoo proclaiming who I was, in much the same way that tap dancing, the art form devoted to the sound of shoes on floors, tells a story with its insistent percussive rhythm.

I could explore the hypothesis that platform shoes—in fact, all shoes—are kinetic sculpture with a noise element, with each shoe style striking a unique chord as it echoes down the hall of fame. That the sounds shoes make add to the effectiveness of an outfit: that the squelch of rubber soles becomes the authoritative tread of nurses, policemen, and gumshoes; that the resonance of soldiers' boots goose-stepping in unison symbolizes fascist power.

Yes, big shoes are attention getting—the same way spinach on your teeth is attention getting.

But I have to admit that, at the time, none of this would have made sense to me. I just thought platforms were cool. (Unfortunately, there is photographic evidence to the contrary. Memories fade, but embarrassing photos hang around forever.) The fact is, I looked a complete and utter idiot.

We all did. It was the seventies.

AN ITALIAN INTERLUDE

· ·

The Good, the Bad, and the Cute

I have happy memories of a shoe store in Rome and an Italian salesman with film star good looks. He worked in a high-class establishment, the kind with oak paneling, many Aubusson rugs, ersatz Louis Quinze coffee tables, hushed lighting, and cathedral-size arrangements of real, living flowers. The staff tread more carefully in the soft splendor of these kinds of stores, and keep their voices lower. It's sort of like being in church, or a very, very expensive beauty salon.

In the seventies, Italy was a truly magical place for shoe lovers. Good leather, reasonable prices, and meticulous craftsmanship—what more could a girl want? I was living in Umbria, passionate about all things Italian, and attempting to become effortlessly bilingual. (A goal I had yet to achieve, although I did

How to Test-Drive Shoes

- In the United States, there is one-sixth of an inch difference in length between half shoe sizes and one third of an inch between full sizes. Most people have one foot slightly smaller than the other. Know which is which and always try on both shoes.
- Do a lap or two around the store. The widest part of the foot should fit comfortably into the widest part of the shoe, because this is where both the foot and the shoe bend. Also check that the back of the shoe (known as the heel counter) holds your own heel snugly, so it doesn't slide up and down while you're walking.
- Try on shoes with stockings or socks. And be aware, if you are buying summer shoes on sale in winter, that your feet are probably a little smaller in winter than in summer. Some people also find that their feet swell toward the end of the day.
- Shoes with genuine leather uppers are better—they don't trap sweat, they conform to the shape of your foot comfortably, and they look classier. Leather soles, however, don't make much difference, except in price. Man-made soles can be very slippery when new, and then should be abraded before wearing to prevent falls. The lining inside a shoe should be smooth and seamless.
- High boots are more difficult to construct than short boots, so they are expensive. Exotic skins such as lizard, ostrich, and alligator are also expensive but much tougher than regular leather and will last a long time.

know a few words of Italian. The essential ones, anyway, like *cappuccino* and *gelato* and *Gucci.*)

I had been drawn into the store by the elegant honey-colored leather heels in the window. When the cute salesman approached I pointed to them. *Sette? Otto?* I hoped my fractured Italian request for size seven or eight sounded adorable and endearing.

Of course, he didn't understand what I was trying to say, but by now I'd become used to this inexplicable phenomenon: the blank stares of the locals when addressed in clear, painstakingly articulated words and phrases in their own language.

The *venditore* summoned up all his English to say something. It sounded as if he was telling me I had beautiful feet. I pronate inward, have chronic little toe calluses, and in those days was innocent of the art of pedicure. That couldn't be right.

He tried pantomime, made eating motions with his fingers. Was this Roman god asking me out? I was flustered. We laughed. I had been, it seemed, magically transported onto the movie set of a cute romantic comedy. Waves of adorableness radiated from him like heat from the Sicilian sun. No other shoe salesman has ever been able to distract me so completely from shoes.

Long story short: Language problems led to a breakdown in communication that stymied this promising interlude. He kept asking me out, asking if I was *erng-ery?*—hungry—but I thought he was asking if I was angry and kept denying it vehemently: *No! Niente! Not at all!*

I'll forever regret that this linguistic misunderstanding

deprived me of a wonderful opportunity for a meaningful relationship with—finally!—a man who understood shoes.

Because while a shoe that is perfect in every way is a rare gem, even more rare are truly helpful shoe salesmen. Shoe divas are invariably fascinating, passionate people, but those who sell shoes are a weird and varied bunch.

A salesman working on commission (instantly recognizable in New York by his effusive and unnatural friendliness) will

Negozio di Calzature

give you several of his business cards and tell you that every pair you try on is absolutely you. He is amazed at the perfection of fit and color—and they also come in navy. This can be somewhat annoying, but is much to be preferred to the salesman who is being paid by the hour and refers to this as his "day job." This guy spends most of his time in the stock-

No other shoe salesman has ever been able to distract me so completely from shoes.

room sitting on a pile of returned twelve narrows, playing poker. When he finally deigns to saunter back to the selling floor, having allegedly hunted everywhere for the divine slingbacks that caught your eye several hours ago, he will call out, *Not in your size, honey!* or *Only comes in puce.* He also takes malicious glee in the sight of a six-and-a-half trying to shoehorn herself into a five.

A good shoe salesman is one who wears a groove in the floor on his endless journeys to the back of the store, muttering, *six triple D, nine narrow, five or five-and-a-half.* He knows that dark blue is not the same as black, and that *a kind of beige-ey color* is not an adequate answer, that he must fetch an actual example of shoes in the color he is attempting to describe.

A good shoe salesman doesn't try to tell a customer that the style she wants is "discontinued" in red suede. He knows that she has no doubt researched this fact for herself, is more conversant with the company's product line than their own chief executives, and is in the process of visiting every shoe store in the tri-state area to track down the red suede.

A good shoe salesman does not hover. He knows you need time to mentally pair those ankle-wrap strappy sandals with everything in your wardrobe. He knows that you are perfectly capable of talking yourself into blowing a week's paycheck on an adorable pair of coffee-colored baby heels with no additional help from him whatsoever.

A good shoe salesman will bring out additional temptations to the ones you requested, just on the off-chance that you may be interested. He will show no impatience at all when you decide against a shoe moments after having declared it absolutely darling. He knows that you must never settle for less than shoes that are not only beautiful themselves, but that make you feel beautiful, too.

I know, I know. Women also sell shoes. But when it comes to love-hate relationships, the anguish of unrequited lust, and the difficulty of finding true love, I tend to think of guys and shoes simultaneously.

A GUY'S SOLE: CLUES FROM THE SHOES

Shoes Make the Man

You can find shoes that look divine or you can find shoes that fit or you can find shoes you can afford, but rarely do all three attributes come together in one pair.

This is also true of men.

Which is why princesses spend a lot of time kissing frogs, and why they frequently create their own personality evaluation tests . . . using shoes. You know you've done it. One glance at those purple patent penny loafers gives you the whole scenario: the dead-end job, the strange sense of humor, the disturbing tendency to idolize John Travolta. A single squint at overembellished cowboy boots, and it all becomes crystal clear: the peacock persona, the maxed-out credit card, the need to see himself as Hopalong Cassidy.

The most telling
evidence of his
basic values
is always his
footwear.

The carrying case a guy chooses for his laptop might be a reliable indication of his sense of style, and the kind of car he drives might signal something psychologically profound about how he sees himself, but the most telling evidence of his basic values is always his footwear. His economic and social status, how much he cares about what others think, the movie star he most identifies with—it's all displayed in his choice of shoe.

Years of dating have led me to one incontrovertible conclusion: it's amazing how much you can tell about a guy on the basis of just that one part of his outfit.

Women can't be pigeonholed the same way. When men assume loose morals on the basis of a tight tube top and gold, wenchy heels, they miss the point. A girl in dangerous glittery stilettos may not necessarily be a va-va-va-voom type. She could actually be wearing therapeutic footwear to boost her down-at-heel self-confidence. The rest of the year, perhaps, she lives in sincere beige flats or shy, gray, suede loafers. As a mirror of what's inside, guy's shoes are a reflection of who they are most of the time, while women's shoes are a reflection of how they're feeling about life right now.

Women have dozens of shoe personalities available in their wardrobes to express themselves—hostile hiking boots, graceful slingbacks, vain comma-heeled pumps, whimsical moccasins, innocent mary janes, ankle boots with attitude, vinyl clogs that are broody, sullen, and withdrawn.

Men tend to be monogamous, shoewise. They usually have one pair they wear day in, day out. They tend to have a total of just four shoe moods, at most, in their closets: loafers, sandals, sneakers, and the wedding-and-funeral shoes they never wear unless they have to.

You no doubt have your own horror stories of gratuitous footwear ugliness and the guys who love it. Techno running shoes that have a lumpy rubber undercarriage in emergency-vehicle acid lime green, worn by spidery young men in vintage T-shirts who are researching alien life-forms. Wheat-colored, lug-soled, four-wheel-drive health sandals worn by brooding

malcontents with ponytails and organic-celery tendencies. Weird monk's-strap-sneaker hybrids fastened by excessive amounts of Velcro, worn by guys who also tend to accessorize with ferrets.

Rugged individualists wear alligator lace-ups; ragged individuals wear lackluster boat shoes. And if luggage-tan brogues are man at his best, scuffed slip-ons (with the back of the shoe pushed inward for even easier slipping on) is man at his messed. To say nothing of such footwear folly as creaky oxblood-colored leather gladiator sandals, very pointy shoes of any kind, lint-trap-gray-colored calf, woven straw and fabric mesh, an overabundance of tassels, or large metal buckles on shoes that are not part of a period costume.

If I had my way, there would be severe legal penalties for wearing white socks with black shoes, or any socks at all with hot-weather huaraches.

However, it's best not to be too harsh. Better to regard a guy's shoe style the way school teachers regard handwriting—quirkiness doesn't necessarily rate an F if everything else checks out, but you get a much better grade for classy presentation.

Rating a person by his shoes can backfire. Throughout my decades of dating I noticed a disturbing, recurring scenario. Whenever I did find a perfect guy—funnier than John Cleese, cuter than Sean Connery, sweeter than a Reese's Peanut Butter

Cup, and wearing made-to-measure hand-sewn driving shoes—there was always one minor but important obstacle to relationship bliss.

Invariably, at the same time as I was checking him out, the guy I was evaluating had the nerve to sum *me* up in a totally unreasonable manner on the basis of some dumb, unrealistic private rating system of his own. Not only that, but to add injury to insult, he usually ended up crossing me off his list and went on his down-at-heel, scuffed-desert-boot way—still on that eternal quest for the perfect woman.

THE MAGIC OF RED SHOES

· ·

The Power and the Gory

I can pinpoint exactly when my aspiration to be art director of *The Tabloid* ended. It was the day Tiny Tim almost died, and also my first time in public in my new cherry-red spike-heeled ankle-straps with silver buckles.

My boss was away, and in his stead I was to attend the afternoon news meeting with the top-of-food-chain editors in the conference room. I arrived early, sat myself near the end of the half-block-long mahogany table, crossed my legs, and assumed the look of someone who was fully capable of coping with a busy night's news graphics single-handedly.

Editors arrived, yellow notepads in hand, generals ready to report on troop positions for tomorrow's battle. The executive

I crossed my legs and assumed the look of someone who was fully capable of coping with a busy night's news graphics single-handedly.

editor (lanky, acerbic, British) began calling on each editor in turn.

"Features!"

The features editor pulled out a list of articles for the next day's paper. "Profile on Madonna . . . Broadway roundup . . . early Oscar predictions. That's about it for tomorrow."

"Sports!" The sports editor responded with an overview of the day's games.

"Financial!" The finance editor read his notes: he was planning stories on the stock market, a big company merger, and the expected impending rate rise.

The only time I'd ever spoken to the executive editor was when he'd complained about a crooked Sunday crossword and I'd aplogized. I was almost hoping that this afternoon he would call out "Sunday crosswords." It occurred to me that if I were truly executive material I would have done more to power-schmooze my way into his consciousness. Never mind, he'd be impressed by my masterly handling of the graphics tonight. Red shoes are the best confidence-builders there are.

The door opened and Mulcahy, the metropolitan news chief, arrived bearing armfuls of rival tabloids, candy, and blustery good cheer. He was a veteran newspaperman from the old press-card-in-the-hatband, *Get me rewrite,* and *Stop the presses* days. Even his hair was the dry, pale sepia of old tabloid pages.

He threw M&M's and photocopied lists of breaking news stories across the expanse of tabletop.

The executive editor picked up a copy of the news list and deliberated down at it. "Not much here, is there?"

"Slow day . . . ," said Mulcahy. "Columbus Day . . ."

"Veteran's day."

"Whatever." Mulcahy cast a worried eye over the barren list himself, then brightened. "We might get lucky. Tiny Tim's in hospital."

"Serious?"

"We're *hoping* he'll be transferred to intensive care. . . ."

"TINY TIM NEAR DEATH," said the executive editor, thinking headlines aloud. Other suggestions flew around the room. "TIM DIMS," "FALSETTO FADES."

Someone who was real executive journalist material—a Brenda Starr girl-reporter type who often wore cherry-red spike-heeled ankle straps with silver buckles—would have been thrilled at the graphic possibilities. But I was beginning to feel slightly nervous.

"I can't *promise* he's gonna die anytime soon," said Mulcahy in an injured tone. "He might take a turn for the *worse*. . . ." He read from the list of news stories. I followed the printed words on the page: "*Fare hike protest scheduled. We're stopping motorists for reactions. Dead Reverend: We're going for the grieving family. Local color."*

"Didn't we just *have* a dead minister last week?" interrupted the executive editor.

"Story's a week old." Mulcahy sounded apologetic. He would have loved to have been able to give the editor a fresh murder. *"A.M. mayhem: Seven injured in Bronx shootout outside illegal social club. Five arrested."*

"Social notes from the Bronx," sneered the finance editor.

"Next item."

"Only wire stories, press conferences, and fillers."

"So what's the wood?" The wood was *The Tabloid*'s front page headline: sassy enough and large enough, in second-coming-of-Christ-size type, to get the attention of commuters hurrying past newsstands at subway entrances. "Anyone?"

Silence.

"Maybe we can make Tiny Tim into something," said the features editor. "Timeline ... cradle to grave ... Could we handle a pullout section on his life's work?"

I tried not to look rattled as faces turned toward me. I knew better than to try to speak: my voice tends to squeak when I panic. A slow day like today meant the editors would have acres of space to fill with complicated graphics, heavily retouched

Even with a closet full of red shoes, this wasn't my dream job.

photos, unusual typefaces. A frenzied five hours to go until the first edition was locked up. You can cope, I told myself. Red shoes have power. Red shoes got Dorothy home to Kansas. But somehow this drama felt more like the movie *The Red Shoes*, where red ballet pumps take on a life of their own and compel Moira Shearer to keep dancing, frenzied and frantic, until her death.

Around me editors were shifting in their seats, suggesting, condemning, agreeing, deriding.

"An aesthete for our time . . ." "Iconoclastic entertainer . . ." "He'll always be alive in our hearts. . . ."

"But is he *dead* yet?" interrupted the executive editor. "Dead, we'd have a story. Why are we guessing here? We're in the *communication* business, and nobody talks to one another. We need an update. . . ."

Mulcahy picked up the phone behind him. During the silence I watched figures move in the glass skyscraper across the street. I knew right then that for me, no matter what happened, and even with a closet full of red shoes, this wasn't my dream job.

"He's okay! What do you mean, he's *okay*?" Mulcahy slumped, defeated. He slammed down the phone and swore. "Sent home from the hospital! Jesus!"

"Well, there's our headline," sighed the executive editor. "TIM'S MIRACULOUS RECOVERY."

BOWS ON EVERYTHING

. . . .

Trying Too Hard

There were good things about the eighties and bad things about the eighties. It was the age of stretch fabrics; it was the age of AIDS. It was the music of Madonna; it was the TV of *Dynasty* and *Dallas*. It was the epoch of leggings and power dressing; it was the epoch of designer logos and big hair. It was the season of feeling old enough to be confident and self-assured; it was the season when fine lines started clawing in around my eyes. It was the spring of my first well-paid job; it was the winter of thinking they had made a terrible mistake in hiring me. I had moments of elation and weeks of despair—in short, I was living in post-fiscal-crisis Manhattan. It was the eighties, and I was in my thirties. I wore linebacker-big padded shoulder suits, read articles titled "Effective Interpersonal

Cheap Frills

These ideas will lead to footwear looks that are either incredibly tacky or incredibly cute—it all depends on your age, your outfit, and your attitude.

Revitalizing old shoes:

- Hammer carpet tacks into soles of an old pair of shoes at the toes and heels (taking care they don't go right through to the inside of the shoe)—instant tap shoes!
- Replace the laces in your lace-up shoes—try a contrasting color.
- Polishing leather shoes with a different color shoe polish can give an interesting "antique" effect. Try black polish on tan shoes, for example. The black will settle in the cracks and tone down the original tan color. Try this, of course, only on shoes that you won't mind tossing if the result is not a good look.

Cheap frills for the young of feet:

- Make a pair of Carmen Miranda beach slippers: buy a pair of inexpensive rubber flip-flops, plus glue suitable for rubber, and some small plastic fruit, flowers, seashells, or what-have-you, and start creating.
- A fresh pair of canvas tennis shoes or slip-ons make a great art canvas for colored felt pens. Create mix-and-match outfits: draw red dots on white shoes to wear with your red clam-diggers with the white dots.
- Browse through a notions shop for embroidered patches (anchors, tiny roses, cartoon figures) or buckles, bows, or sequins, to glue onto a fabric shoe.
- Wander through Chinatown for inexpensive footwear, such as flat embroidered satin slippers and clear plastic jelly sandals.

Motivational Techniques and Management Models," and mistakenly believed I had achieved something, careerwise. My own personal economy was revving up, and I bought shoes.

In fact, all my friends bought shoes, but especially Ned, who had—still has—the most distinctive aesthetic and unerring taste of anyone I've ever known. I worshiped the ground her lime-green mary janes tap-danced over. The same bright, glittering promise of New York had drawn us both with its irresistible centrifugal pull—me from the other side of the world, Ned from Alpine, Texas. We worshiped Diana Vreeland and devoted a good proportion of our time, effort, and shoe money to creating pizzazz.

Ned did pizzazz magnificently, and with her beautiful posture and serene self-confidence could carry off even the most outrageous outfit. She found patent leather shoes covered in buttons, and made a matching dress. She wore black shoes with white polka dots and red heels and looked sensational. She made a skirt out of thrift-store neckties and got me to photograph her in front of a Madison Avenue church where the posted sermon was "Blest be the ties." She owned bright orange suede oxfords and Calvin Klein two-tone wingtips. She was style personified.

And where she trod, I attempted to follow. Or rather, I skittered in her wake, trying to keep up. I, too, wore shoes that

With big fat juicy markers I
gave the white pair navy bows.

made a statement. Not, however, a fashion statement.

I fell in love with the look of D'Orsay pumps but fell out of the cutaway sides. I spent a lot of money on ghillie lace-ups before I fully realized how unbecoming they are. I bought glorious black suede flats with the word *left* embroidered in gold san serif letters on the right shoe, the word *right* stitched on the left. (Their magnificence was only slightly dimmed by the minor disappointment of not being able to fully admire oneself without a complicated system of mirrors, since the script faced the wrong way.)

These were shoes that on Ned would indicate an elegant sense of humor and inimitable style. On me they indicated an attention-deficit disorder and inability to tell left from right. The shoes were so *her* that I hardly ever wore them, finally gave them to their rightful owner, and went out the next day to trawl for new treasure. Manhattan was my stage and my playground, my workshop and the backyard I scrounged around for raw materials.

Ned outstyled me at every turn, but I never gave up trying, and was always on the look-out for funky fashion fabulousness. One day, in Lord & Taylor, I came across a chorus line of colored shoes with large, puffy grosgrain bows on the front. Wow! Huge mix-and-match potential.

I bought two pairs, red and white. With big fat juicy mark-

The shoes died beneath me,
right there and then, in the
middle of Fifth Avenue.

ers I gave the white pair navy bows, the red pair black bows. The effect was part music hall, part Minnie Mouse, and altogether ridiculous. I thought they had pizzazz.

I wore the blue-and-whites with a sailor outfit and turned more than a few heads when I showed up at work in the ensemble, a reaction I mistook for envy. I often wondered whether the comments it inspired—comments like "Well, look at you!"—were compliments or not. For years I believed I looked mighty fetching in my home-dyed shoes, right up until the day I was crossing Fifth Avenue next to a nice-looking stranger whose eyes had locked on to my footwear—with admiration, I assumed, until I noticed the expression on his face and heard him say rhetorically, "You did that yourself, didn't you?"

The shoes died beneath me, right there and then, in the middle of Fifth Avenue. Suddenly they were a pathetic, loving-hands-at-home attempt at creativity, a big expensive mistake, the product of a tortured, fashion-fractured mind. I felt like the emperor must have felt when the villagers finally believed their eyes and told him he had no clothes on.

During the eighties, I tried pizzazz and discovered that pizzazz was not my best look.

(But it was a lot of fun trying.)

FOOTWEAR FOLLIES

. . . .

How to Resist Temptation

For most healthy people, shoe sales cause only short-term problems. But for individuals with weakened immune systems (those suffering from work-related worries, hormone inharmony, or recently broken hearts), a really good sale can cause an immediate increase in the pulse rate and long-term budget-related problems.

Over the years I have given a lot of thought to how to avoid these pitfalls in the purchasing process. At one stage in my shoe-buying career, I decided that to successfully rationalize acquiring yet another pair, I'd succumb only if they produced Overwhelming Adoration—that jagged peak of ecstasy, that heart-stopping thrill that you'd pay money for at an amuse-

How to Stretch Shoes That Are Too Small

(But Were So Beautiful You Had to Buy Them)

The amount a shoe can be stretched depends on the type of shoe, what it's made of, and how much it has to be stretched.

If the uppers of a shoe are made of unlined leather, they will stretch more easily than those of lined leather or man-made materials. Even without stretching, unlined leather will, over time, conform to the shape of your foot.

You can stretch shoes that are just a little tight by wearing them with thick socks around the house.

For more drastic stretching, buy a shoe-stretcher from a shoe repair shop and use with liquid shoe-stretch spray (a leather softening liquid). Or go to a good cobbler who has an appliance that applies force and heat to a specific part of the shoe.

ment park, that immobilizing bliss that happens only when you've found your true love.

Another strategy was to make myself take a time-out before I committed to a big-ticket buy. It seemed that the more impulsive a purchase, the bigger mistake it turned out to be, that the half-life of an immediate must-have was usually very short and sorry. (And my feet were the ones who ended up most sorry.)

These How-to-Talk-Yourself-Out-of-a-Shoe Guidelines, designed to lower the incidence of post-purchase remorse, are the result of decades of shopping experience and the mistakes it produced: The pair of authentic, Italian, rope-soled espadrilles that gave my own soles authentic, painful rope burn. The expensive blue sandals bought to go with all my denim clothes but went with none of them, even the ones I bought later, in desperation, especially to go with the shoes. The clear, see-through plastic pumps that turned clammy and opaque with perspiration. The dirt-magnet satin mules that were too much of a bargain to pass up.

Take it from a veteran shopper—these guidelines will help:

· How to talk yourself out of shoes that are impractical and frivolous and expensive but wonderful: A few tough questions should do it: Did you know this morning, before seeing these hot-pink snakeskin stilettos, that they were all it took to make your life complete and meaningful? Will they be a wardrobe staple? Can you, in fact, think of any outfit you currently own that they will complement perfectly? Are you often required to attend functions where hot-pink snakeskin would be the only suitable shoes to wear? I thought as much. (However, if you are prepared to reedit your wardrobe so that it revolves around hot-pink snakeskin, these shoes could add a whole new dimension to your life.)

SHOP SALE

25% OFF

A really good sale can cause an immediate increase in the pulse rate and long-term budget-related problems.

• **How to justify shoes that are so outrageously expensive that you tremble as you hand over the credit card:** The only extenuating circumstance here is that you wholeheartedly adore these shoes and can unhesitatingly promise to wear them forever and ever, until death do you part. I'm not talking *They're almost what I was looking for* or *They'll do for now* or, heaven forbid, *They'll stretch.* (However, if you've just been given a bonus or in some other way deserve a little retail therapy, buy them without guilt. Life is short.)

• **How to talk yourself out of shoes that are absolutely perfect but are, if you're going to be gut-wrenchingly honest, too small:** Remember that corns on your toes mean never being able to wear sandals again, to say nothing of blisters, calluses, and foot, leg, and back pain. (But before you give up all hope, ask the sales clerk if she can put in a special order or telephone other branches of the store to find a larger size. Or make a note of the manufacturer, see if they have a Web site, and e-mail your request to it. If we're talking about a seize-the-moment situation, however, and you really love them, get them and take them to a good cobbler—miracles have been known to happen by stretching.)

• **How to evaluate shoes that are not quite what you wanted but have a designer label and are 25 percent off:** Decide which of the three is more important to you—looks, comfort, or price. Give the shoes a rating in each category. Why not wait for a pair that score ten out of ten in all three? Or calculate the probable Number of Wearings Divided into Cost—can you can live with three wearings at twenty dollars each? (On the other hand—or foot—can you really pass up that pair of Carmen Miranda beach casuals for only twenty-five dollars?)

• **How to weed out the Wants from the Needs:** Are these shoes really you, or just the you you wish you were . . . but aren't? If you had to evacuate your home and could escape only in the shoes you were wearing, would these fringed pirate boots at least be on the short list? Is this yet another evening-only sandal when your wardrobe already has

If they're on sale, buy 'em.

more than its share of yummy after-hours indulgences and hardly any meat-and-potatoes pumps for work? (However, it's important to be prepared for any eventuality. Even if you don't really need those rhinestone-buckled denim slides—if they're on sale, buy 'em.)

BEST FOOT FORWARD

. . . .

Indecision Time

The need to give good shoe—it's in my genes. (Every shoe junkie has her own excuse.) Maybe it started at the feet of my mother, who found it necessary to change her shoes even to answer the front door. The pizza delivery guy, the postman—heaven forbid they should see her in well-worn corduroy casuals.

In my case, the affliction manifests itself as chronic indecision. Each time I open my closet, I have a problem choosing which shoes to wear. On a good shoe day, it's because every pair is just so incredibly wonderful. On a bad shoe day, it's more complicated—the recently purchased are too good to actually *wear*, yet the tribal elders have passed their amuse-by date. I don't want to scuff up any of the shoes I absolutely adore, but the comfy ones that make sense because I'll be on my feet all day don't really go with anything in my closet. And on really, *really* bad shoe days, nothing I slip into looks right, and there's really no point in living any longer. In short, it's entirely possible to waste twenty minutes of a manic morning in stressful scavenging at the back of the closet.

Big evenings out are even worse. I feel compelled to parade six different pairs of shoes before my loved one in a kind of footwear talent quest in which I ask him which stilettos he prefers, these or the pink, over and over, until I sound like a crazed optometrist. (*Is it better this way? Or this? This one . . . or this?*) I'm just trying to narrow it down to the finalists before selecting a winner, but I manage to make him feel trapped in a nightmare. He knows that *Which pair are your favorites?* is one of those trick girly questions, like *Can you tell I've lost weight?* or *Why don't you ever talk to me?* and he has no idea how to respond. I know I've chosen the worst possible time for an attack of shoe-indecision and we start fighting on what was meant to be a pleasant, relaxing evening. Chronic shoe-aholic insecurity strikes again.

During the eighties, I thought lists were the answer. (Is anyone else that obsessive? To devote an evening in front of the full-length mirror, pencil in hand, working out once and for all exactly what heel height is the perfect amount of eleva-

On really, really bad shoe days, when nothing I slip into looks right, there's really no point in living any longer.

tion beneath boot-cut Levi's, which pair of black pumps make the ideal marriage with the Little Black Evening Dress, composing ideal-world shoe scenarios, deciding what goes with what and getting it all down on paper via sketches, diagrams, and cryptic descriptions?)

But lists don't work.

Oh, maybe they do for a week, but then they don't, because in a few days it gets colder or warmer or wetter and you have to rethink the whole thing since, as everyone knows, when it comes to shoes there are quite a different number of seasons than are generally allowed for. Some may last only a few days, but you still need to be prepared for them with the appropriate foot attire. For example, in the semitropical climate where I grew up, there were three seasons: sturdy-shoe winter, flip-flop heat, and the very tricky waterproof-but-cool-footwear-for-summer-monsoon-downpour months. In New York, of course, there are at least six seasons: new-fall-loafer chilliness; boot weather;

Powerful alligator pumps that say,
The real me has a window office.

extra warm, fleecy-lined boot weather; emergency-April-shower wear; then an all-too-soon-over pretty-spring-sandal week followed quickly by tar-melting summer-slide dog days.

And, to complicate matters, sometimes shoes mysteriously and viciously turn against you. Platypus-toed mary janes that once looked snub-nosed and pixie cute are now, inexplicably, dull-witted and dorky, and especially surly before noon—good shoes gone bad for no apparent reason. The floral fabric flats that usually make you feel girly and summery metamorphose, overnight, into faux pas footwear. The chisel-toed oxfords that were so elegant when you bought them a week ago, today give you the cloven hooves of a cartoon character. Casual style can become style casualty at the drop of a mood swing.

I've found, however, there's one small scrap of wisdom that helps. *Make footwear decisions based on how you want people to respond to you.* I've taped this up inside my shoe closet. It means thinking about who you want to appear to be, and conveying that message in a subliminal way. Your shoes can not only be appropriate for the occasion and the weather but can also display any emotion you want your audience to feel. Contempt, pity, envy—it's all possible with the right shoes. Your footwear can proclaim you to be audacious (red boots), declare your innocence (white ballet slippers), or tell the world to go take a hike (aggressive Doc Martens). You can choose powerful alligator pumps that say *The real me has a window office* or twinkly wraparound strappy sandals that say *I expect to be ravished this evening.* (It's a lot for a pair of pumps to say, but if you are a true shoe diva, you know they can say it.)

Someone once said that the sense of being well dressed provides a feeling of inward tranquillity that religion is powerless to bestow. It's so true, and I love that feeling. I just have to decide which shoes will give it to me today.

MEN VS. SHOES

. . . .

Putting Them Through Their Paces

Yes, I've lost men over shoes. Or, more accurately, shoe shopping.

In fact, as a first-date test, you can't beat a shoe store. You're walking home after the movies or on the way to dinner. Do this: slow down in front of a Parade of Shoes. The guys who pull on your leash at the merest hint that you might want to sniff out a SALE sign are sure to be trouble. I cross them off my list immediately, no matter how Trustworthy, Loyal, Helpful, Friendly, Courteous, Kind, Obedient, Cheerful, Thrifty, Brave, Clean, and Reverent they may otherwise be.

Unfortunately, it's not easy to find a guy who considers acquiring footwear a fun activity. Suggest a visit to the nearest cut-price designer shoe outlet to a potential boyfriend and watch his brave smile dissolve into polite misgiving. Tell him about an end-of-season, two-for-the-price-of-one, summer sandal event and see his expression take on a deeper melancholy. It's a truth universally acknowledged: Men buy, women shop.

Most men rate shoe shopping somewhere between cleaning up after the dog and a visit to the dentist. A man will go to his wedding with the sole of one shoe held on with duct tape. Men don't know that, like cholesterol, there's good shopping and bad shopping. They don't know the joys of going out for half a pound of tomatoes and coming home with a pair of adorable candy-colored lizard heels, size seven; or the thrill of delivering that in-your-dreams line: *I'll take a pair in every color.*

It's like this: Women have always been the gatherers of the tribe. Over the millennia, while the guys were out there spearing

The guys who pull on your leash at the merest hint that you might want to sniff out a SALE sign are sure to be trouble.

antelope—the kind of big and obvious actions they still take pride in—the women specialized in digging around in the undergrowth for a few tasty nuts and berries, ferreting out a great little grove of fennel by the river or patiently picking over the mussels at the seashore. Searching and gathering have been bred into our psyches over eons, so no wonder it's kind of hard to get out of the system. The fact that you have, oh, maybe twelve pairs of black pumps at home is immaterial when you see an absolute honey of a pair in a shop window. It's physiological—women are programmed to forage for the perfect black pump forever.

Our baby-making years, however, are limited. During my late thirties I became conscious that some of my favorite shoes had lasted longer than any of my relationships. (It helped put things in perspective.) I probably hold a world record for number of years dating—love comes and goes, but shoes are true lust. In my forties, some of my friends were becoming grandmothers, and I was still looking for someone who didn't go all squirrely when he discovered just how many occupied shoe boxes were lurking under my bed.

I don't ask for much, just tolerance: a guy who sees owning sixty-two pairs of shoes as a harmless hobby rather than something more closely resembling a personality disorder; a guy who doesn't assume that the presence of a closet crammed with nothing else but shoes is a marker for a cluster of genetically linked traits, all of them connected with neurotic behavior and pathological attachment.

Against all odds, I finally found someone wonderful in my forties, after I'd just about resigned myself to remaining single in a world full of emotionally commitment-averse misfits, marginally psychotic jerks, and footwear-hating shoe-a-phobics.

On my first date with the love of my life, he asked, *Can you walk in those shoes?* I assumed he felt the same way I did—that the ice-blue beaded stilettos I had on were far too beautiful to ruin when there were plenty of taxis available. Later, he admitted everything: *I just wanted to forestall the inevitable breakdown. I've seen it all too often. Women buy shoes that are too small—one block, they go to pieces. I can't stand it.*

But we have both persevered. There are two things I love about this man. One, he's an enabler. He hands me Band-Aids (blister protection) when I insist on wearing new shoes immediately. He aids and abets me in shoe-related craft projects, such as re-creating the bedroom bunny slippers of my babyhood. And he knows that *You look great in those, buy them*, said early and often enough, will save both of us a lot of anguish and heartbreak.

Two, he's a normal guy when it comes to footwear. He doesn't feel the need to own more than six pairs of shoes. Think of the huge advantage here, if ever we decide to join, for better or for worse, our lives, our saucepans, and especially our closets.

I'll get to use his share of the shoe space.

FLIP-FLOPPING ABOUT PEDICURES

Grooming's Open Season

At art college I had a teacher who looked askance at painted fingernails. *Real artists,* she said, *don't have manicures.* At the time, being unable to apply colored lacquer seemed a terrible deprivation—now it's a wonderful excuse. One less body part to tend to.

As time goes on, getting your appearance together and keeping it together isn't just your part-time job, it's your *labor-intensive* part-time job.

It's bad enough having to worry about maintaining a presentable facade (no visible panty lines, seamlessly blended foundation, un-worn-down shoe heels) let alone worrying about the general upkeep of the infrastructure (decreasing your body fat

Caring for Shoes

- Don't drive in high heels. Not only do you have less control, but, much worse, you can also damage the back of your shoe.
- Suede is more fragile than regular leather. Rub very soft suede with a bath towel to bring up the nap, or use masking tape. Those wire brushes sold as suede brushes are useful only on sturdy suede or nubuck; they can be too scratchy for delicate suede. Real shoe-aholics take off their suede shoes, cover them up, and carry them at the first sprinkles of rain; wimps apply silicone weatherproofing spray before wearing them the first time.
- Drying shoes in artificial heat or sunlight can ruin leather and make the soles and uppers separate.
- Clean patent leather shoes by rubbing petroleum jelly into them. Give this a few hours to penetrate, then shine up with a soft clean cloth.
- To shine shoes: Find yesterday's newspaper, an old, overlaundered T-shirt torn into squares, and some paste shoe polish, the kind that comes in a round tin in a color that matches the color of the shoes. A shoe-shine brush and a chamois are useful but not essential.
- Wipe dirt and dust off the shoes with a damp cloth. With a dry cloth, dab on the polish, smearing it all over the shoes except for the soles. Leave the shoes on the newspaper for about fifteen minutes. When the polish has dried, either wipe it off with a cloth or brush it away with the shoe-shine brush. (If the shoe leather is very delicate, skip the brush and go straight to the polishing cloth.) Then make the shoes really shiny by rubbing furiously with a clean cloth or chamois, if you have it.

ratio, keeping yourself adequately hydrated, the on-going battle against free radicals.)

Life ought to get easier. By forty-five, one ought to be the kind of grown-up who applies shoe polish to shoes regularly and can always find her car keys. Not only should everything get done easily and on time, but with flair and sophistication. Decades of practice ought to count for something.

But in reality, the older you get, the harder you have to run just to stay in the same place. You get thrown a lot of additional handicaps, like declining muscle tone and teenage offspring, and find that you've lost a few key attributes along the way, attributes that you'd counted on and taken for granted, like your ability to remember things and your graceful agility in stilettos.

The deterioration starts from the ground and works its way up: The years of living dangerously—pointy-tip pumps, too-tight toe boxes, skyscraper heels—mean you no longer have wispy-ribbon-sandal-quality toes. Rather than becoming routine, simple basic foot maintenance now requires the level of commitment and self-discipline of a military maneuver. The scars of time accumulate faster and faster until getting up and perfectly groomed by 7 A.M. becomes an outstanding personal achievement.

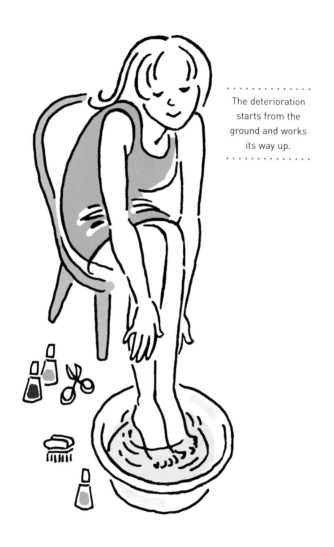

The deterioration starts from the ground and works its way up.

In my early forties, in an effort to simplify, I decided to give up sandals. Perhaps this was motivated by a chance sighting of the crusty soles and ropy veins of my bare feet in close proximity to those of a seventeen-year-old, resulting in a very effective visual definition of the terms *bunions, corns, hammer toes, in-grown toenails,* and *calluses.*

But it was a major turning point that wouldn't stay turned. Pretty shoes are hard to give up. Although I now possessed a gnarly-footed exterior, I still had a strappy-sandal soul. And the moment I decided my feet were too nasty for open-toed shoes there were the most beautiful pairs wherever I looked. I could easily have succumbed to barely there styles with inadequate wisps of leather decorating the front if only they didn't look incongruous with wrinkly skin and curled-caterpillar toes.

Okay—compromise. I tried to find open-toed sandals that would cover, at the very least, my stiletto-crippled toes, mangled by a lifetime of making do with a size medium when I should have held out for a wide. They also had to have a sole sturdy enough to stand up to the tarry reality of city streets in summer.

And then—uh-oh—I recognized what this was: one of the first of the thirty-nine Telltale Signs of Aging. A tendency to buy sensible shoes. Something inside rebelled. It occurred to

I am too
busy living.

me that I was reacting to getting older in the wrong way. I should free myself from the strictures of trying to always look perfect rather than worrying what people thought.

Herewith, my personal list of grooming rationalizations for your own twilight years. Cut out this helpful guide, keep it on the refrigerator, and remember that you are not alone.

- Absolutely meticulous grooming is scary. Think of flight attendants in the early airline decades, or advertisements from the 1950s showing housewives vacuuming in high heels. These women look as sincere as a billboard, inaccessible and aloof.
- A little disarray is sexy. Less is more, as one ages. Less makeup, less extreme heel heights, less harsh lines.
- A woman who spends most of her waking hours worrying about whether her ankles are too wrinkly is a woman who doesn't have any time left over for worrying about mergers and acquisitions or whether her child is ingesting enough vitamin B or if she'll catch the sunset tonight. It's more attractive to have a life than to look as if you spend most of your time obsessing over whether the color of your nail polish is a perfect match with your sandals.
- Repeat after me: I have better things to do than grasp at the last vestiges of youth. I am too busy living.

DUMPING LOVED ONES

. . . .

Discarding Past Personalities

Apart from pulling on a brand-new pair of pure white tennis shoes, replacing all the grouting in the bathroom, or finally scraping all the burnt raisin-bread raisins out of the toaster, there are few experiences as refreshing and soul-cleansing as getting rid of household junk so that you can buy more. Shoes, of course, are not junk. Terrorism, hurricanes, and acts of God can't part a true Imelda from her shoes. Only moving house can do that.

I started the new millennium in a new apartment in another city and discovered just how brutally painful it can be to say good-bye to loved ones.

At first, I was optimistic. This was a chance to start afresh—to

What a Cobbler Can—and Can't—Do

Not all shoe repair stores are the same. The little place in the mall that also cuts keys and engraves tags may be capable only of replacing worn soles. To treat good shoes with respect you need, ideally, to find an artisan: someone who loves leather and has had a lot of experience working with it. The right cobbler can work wonders.

- The height of a heel can usually be increased or decreased about a quarter of an inch. It depends on the shoe's construction, the shape of the heel, and what it is made of. If you are having a heel lowered, try to visualize whether this would make the toe of the shoe turn up, not always an attractive look.
- If the inner sole of a shoe gets stained or smelly, it can usually be easily replaced.
- Outer soles are easily replaced, too. While you are having this done, think about whether you'd like the sole thicker or thinner or smoother or grippier than the one that's currently on there.
- Shoes can be dyed a darker color, but some materials take dye better than others. Take a sample of the color you'd like the shoes to be—someone else's idea of what the word "navy" means may not be the same as yours. And learn from those of us who have had bad experiences with do-it-yourself products: unless you are just having fun with cheap shoes, get a professional to do the dyeing.
- Boots can often be shortened at the top, their zippers can be fixed, and the width of the calf made wider or narrower.
- Seams that have unraveled or torn open can often be fixed. On lace-up shoes, broken hooks and lost eyelets can be replaced.
- Talk to a good cobbler about stretching shoes and boots, especially if there is just one annoying tight area.

Beyond help:

- Small tears, cuts, and scratches can be fixed, but if the leather on the top of a shoe is thin or damaged—cracked, mildewed, or flabby from repeated bending—it's time to give these babies a decent burial.
- Many shoes have a shank, a stiff piece of metal or plastic that runs along the instep. If this breaks, the shoe is beyond heroic measures.
- It's usually not worth replacing the soles on cheap shoes, especially if it would be easy to buy a similar style.

dump the shoes I never wore, toss every pair that didn't quite work. I was determined to keep only the good friends I truly loved.

Out came the whole tangled heap from the back of the closet: The green flats that were too small after all. The Day-Glo pink slingbacks from when I had my colors done in the eighties. The elderly but still cheerful tie-dyed sneaks. The rhinestone-encrusted wedgies that I lived to regret. The trendy turquoise T-straps that bit into my arches at each step. (All perfect when I bought them, all have-to-haves at the point of purchase.)

Two big brown shopping bags later, I could see the floor of my closet for the first time since I moved in.

At this point I attempted to weed out the obvious mistakes. (It was embarrassing to see how many of these there were.) Why hadn't I learned never to go native from the Japanese *waraji* sandals made from rice straw? I didn't even try them on before I bought them—I don't know how to say *Does that come in a seven and a half wide?* in Japanese. Anyway, it didn't matter. I never really expected to wear them—the appeal was purely visual: they looked so exotic hanging on the wall of the shop in Osaka. But somehow, on my wall at home, the *waraji* didn't give off the hoped-for air of ethnic-chic bohemian style. Their message translated from the Japanese as *pathetic attempt to decorate using dusty old bits of dried-out vegetable matter.*

But I'd persisted in falling in love with foreigners. On the same trip I was tempted by a unique pair of geta, the tradi-

I left three pairs of these
might-have-beens
in the co-op's trash room
and felt as if I were
leaving my diary open
for all to read.

tional wooden flip-flops with two little stilts underneath. Each one was the shape of half a pie—put your feet together in them and you were standing on a circle of wood. Cute! Totally unwearable, of course, but cute.

There were also false friends I'd met at home, of course: The pants shoes that were all wrong with pants. The party shoes with the slippery soles that skidded alarmingly on the dance floor. The boots that looked sturdy and reliable but leaked with the first drop of rain. The homely high-throated loafers that turned out to be miserable, moody companions determined to drag me down into depression.

I should have been ruthless at this point. Instead, I started wondering . . . Could any of these marriages be saved? What about "repurposing"? Maybe I should save some pairs to wear in the rain. (*But I already have four other pairs of worn-out shoes that I don't wear when its raining.*) What about saving some for Halloween? Or dyeing. (*But I've been down that road already, and remember the stages: Denial—how difficult can it be to dye shoes? Anger—Aaagh! This color isn't right! And, finally, Acceptance— perhaps nobody'll notice. . . .*) What about giving them to charity? (*Would the deserving poor catered to by my local Goodwill be as thrilled with the two-inch platforms with faux leopardskin-print inner soles as I had been when I first caught sight of them?*)

I left three pairs of these might-have-beens in the co-op's

trash room and felt as if I were leaving my diary open for all to read. So I went back and retrieved them. Then I put them back out. And rescued them again. About ten times—talk about separation anxiety.

If I couldn't get rid of shoes I was positive I would never wear again, how could I abandon the merely elderly? Getting rid of these—steadfast friends that had given support, literally and figuratively, through the years—turned out to be a task worse than abandoning kittens.

The best shoes had miles of my life worn into them. My footprints were imprinted inside by countless wearings. They had been around for decades, through thick and thin soles, for thousands of small journeys. They had molded themselves into comfortable contours and taken on the shape of me, giving them a vulnerability that was impossible to walk away from. Unthinkable to toss them out with the Frosted Flakes cartons.

Could they be saved by the repair gnome on Forty-seventh Street? At what point do you decide *no heroic measures?*

Why is it so hard to throw out shoes? Perhaps because they represent the whole multiple-personality-disorder of past personae I've jettisoned. Little deaths along the way. No longer was I an Executive Barbie in career-girl pumps, or a long-haired center-parted-hair hippie in ridiculous wooden platform soles, or a party girl in sequined raw silk ankle-strap heels. It's difficult to toss out memories

of who you once were, even though you know you'll never return to those past stages of your life.

One must take time to mourn the shoes and the lives you've gone through. Then go out and find new ones.

FOOT FASHION OR FOOT ASSASSIN?

Modern Maturity

In the late nineties I became impatient with pain. I wanted comfort, and I wanted it now. No more midday meltdown. No more blisters and corns and aching feet. No more ouch shoes. Been through spikes. Done slings. Hobbled on.

Remember the movie *Working Girl?* Remember how, in the eighties, women would emerge at a run from mass transit, all wearing business suits, briefcases, and sneakers, defying the fashion police in big rubber boots worn below suits, under overcoats and even accessorizing minks? But some of us in New York—especially those of us who were born in the suburbs—had always resisted the temptation. This was *New York,* for heaven's sake. We'd fought so hard to get here, were struggling so hard to make it, and our New York chic was one of

Feel-Good Fix-Ups for Fatigued Feet

The problem with constantly wearing high heels is that your calf muscles and Achilles tendons (the fibers that connect the calf muscles to the backs of the heels) can become permanently shortened and stiff. If you wear stilettos often, get into a daily habit of exercising and stretching the calf muscles before you put on heels. (If dancers can be disciplined enough to do it, so can you!)

- Sitting on the floor with feet straight out in front of you, point your toes, then flex them back toward you. Bend over and touch your toes, or come as close to it as you can. Don't jerk—breathe in and out slowly and with each out breath sink into the stretch a little more.
- Rotate your feet from the ankles as if making circles, both clockwise and counterclockwise. Spread out your toes as much as you can, straining to move them far apart from each other, then relax.
- And whenever you are sitting—at your desk at work, at a lunch or function—kick off your shoes. The less time spent in pointed toes and high heels, the better.

At the end of a long day, soothe feet by soaking them in water. Try these methods:

- Find two containers large enough to take your feet. Fill one with hot water, one with icy water. Soak feet first in one, then the other. Repeat.
- Or, use just one container, fill it with warm water, and add a tablespoon of milk powder. Add some smooth pebbles for your feet to play with. The milk powder is good for the skin; the pebbles are meant to massage and exercise your feet.

* Lie on your back on the floor or bed with legs up, resting on a wall, so your body makes an L-shape. This provides a surge of fresh blood to your feet when you are vertical again.
* Sit with one foot on the knee of the other leg. Apply a rich moisturizer, and use your thumbs to massage the sole of your foot. Put on cotton socks. Relax.

the few outward and visible signs that we belonged. We clung to style, to heels, our self-respect. But our feet were not happy about it.

After twenty years of pounding New York pavements, even previously comfortable pumps were letting me down—great for a few blocks but no longer first choice for a hike from the Village to Saks, a trek from Bloomies to the West Side. (In Manhattan, one tends to walk a lot—even the well-wheeled go to their corner deli on foot.)

After much agonizing, I'd thrown out almost the entire contents of my current shoe boxes, a towering stack of pain and regrets and blisters. I had only two pairs of shoes to wear out of the house. For a while I was in denial. At home, I lived in slippers, the stretch limo of slippers: Australian shearling-leather Ugg boots. Comforting, but only an indoor solution.

Cost would be no object, I decided. There must exist well-made shoes where fashion and comfort coexisted in harmony.

I began with the high-end shoe stores. For many years, a lean wardrobe budget meant haunting the half-price bins near the entrance of discount stores. Obviously, cheap shoes had caused the foot problems that developed within a few months of wearing anything new. This time I bought expensive, quality brands and noticed the difference—the foot problems started immediately.

Gravity-defying, toothpick-thin heels rammed my protesting toes. Pointy patent-leather python-prints pinched. Five-hundred-dollar needlenose spikes, so sharp you could etch glass with them, crippled.

As recently as the year before, my shoe mantra had been, *The higher the heel, the nearer to heaven.* Now, anything that looked pretty hurt. I asked a clerk at a pricey store for something comfortable and watched the thought balloon form

In the eighties, women would emerge at a run from mass transit, all with briefcases and wearing business suits and sneakers, defying the fashion police.

over her head: *Oh, just give up, already. Go buy yourself some old-lady shoes and join the grannies on the sidelines where you belong.*

The humiliation! But I was determined to resist style oblivion. I do not intend to spend my sunset years in shapeless droopy cardigans and fleecy-lined padded-polyester foam fluff-scuffs.

Surreptitiously I scrutinized the ads for podiatrists in the subway and hung round Dr. Scholl's displays at drugstores, a reluctant student of corn cushions, gel arch supports, and squishy innersoles. *Uuuugh.* Packages labeled ORTHOPEDIC. The obscenities of the old. This couldn't be me, not yet. I furtively acquired bits of foam rubber to stuff inside my few remaining pairs of pumps, and scared myself with a depressing fast-forward of what would come next: earnest conversations with other oldsters about bunions and stiffening body parts. Creeping geezerhood. Toilet-bowl-cleanser-blue helmet hair, expandable elasticized waistbands, polyester separates, and big boats on my feet: the wandered-away-from-the-*Modern-Maturity*-package-tour ensemble.

Meanwhile, magazines were reporting that the walking-challenged who can afford it are getting podiatrists to inject collagen into the balls of their feet so that they will find it more comfortable to wear heels . . . but, eeuch!

I was at an impasse, caught at the fork in the road where

fashion and comfort diverge. There seemed to be only two choices: become the foot equivalent of Tammy Faye Bakker, desperately trying to grab just a little more playing time by hobbling along on ever higher heels, or go straight to the Eleanor Roosevelt old-lady look in sports utility clodhoppers with Velcro fastenings, suitable for grappling up rugged mountain ranges.

Either way, it was good-bye to male attention, female envy, my last vestiges of self-confidence, and any personal sense of style.

A normal person just has a midlife crisis. A shoe addict suffers the additional agonies of Ugly-Footwear Angst, Stiletto Deprivation Syndrome, and Schlumpy Sneaker Shellshock.

For a while I was in denial.
At home, I lived in slippers.

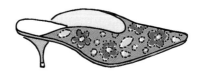

TIME SLIDES BY

· ·

Mule Strain

This morning I had all the shoes I needed. Now I am standing in front of the most beautiful slides in the world, transfixed. Embroidered toes, graceful shape, kitten heel—I can't tell you how much I long to have them.

If I owned these mules, I'd be the sort of person I want to be: a cool, sophisticated diva, elegant but not loud, fascinating but not boastful; a person who travels to interesting places and has delightful experiences. These mules promise to provide all the excitement my life is currently lacking. I pick one up, immobile with desperation and desire. Who says you can't buy happiness?

The new-shoe-glue smell is a powerful aphrodisiac. My size fits divinely. I stand up and instantly feel glamorous, taller—a new sassy me. Even in a ratty old T-shirt and ripped jeans, I feel a million times more beautiful than a moment before. The applause of heel slapping against shoe follows me back and forth in front of the mirror. I am transformed from Rosa Klebb into Heidi Klum.

Tidal waves of primordial yearning wash over me: I want . . . I want . . . I want . . .

These are exactly the yearnings I had resolved to give up for the rest of my life. This year was going to mark the end of impractical shoes. Sense must prevail. The pain crisis was followed by several months of careful buying and rigorous editing, resulting in a satisfactory, but subdued, shoe wardrobe. My current pairs can be cataloged into a few Cool Sophisticate numbers (four pairs of black pumps in gradations of fabulousness), a larger Smart-Casual division (loafers and sandals with enough of a heel to look elegant), and a small but quirky Lovable Eccentric section (Hawaiian print fabric flats, polka-dot rain boots). This is the current me. I love these shoes, I love what they say about me. I can be myself in them; they are all I really need. I'm flirting with a toxic relationship, now, falling in love with shoes I know will be uncomfortable. The slides I'm holding represent a step backwards in my evolution.

But I can no more stop myself wanting these shoes than I can wanting to breathe. I miss the deep pleasure and instant gratification of loving a pair of shoes so much that you have to walk out of the shop in them, that you have to claim them immediately as part of yourself.

Should I get them? My inner voice jumps back and forth between reasonable, rational objections and greedy whining. I can't help feeling that a more highly evolved, less self-centered person would feel this euphoria about more worthy, intellectual productions—Shakespeare, perhaps, the ballet, or opera.

But there are worse things one can be addicted to. And these mules make me happy. I buy them. I take them home. I spend a lot of time staring at them. On me, heelless slides slap around like bedroom slippers—try running up stairs in these babies, or worse, down! I fall off Louis heel slingbacks when I run for the bus, and these have even less support. They give new meaning to the word *slipshod*.

A lot of soul-searching goes on. I grudgingly admit these shoes would have only a walk-on part to play in my life. I try them on again, feel their silky sleekness one last time, then fold them back into the tissue paper in their box. I decide not to risk life and limb and hip replacements.

I'm coping with getting older. I'm evolving. I'm setting myself new goals: I'm on a quest for the perfect designer sneaker-type shoe. I read that Nike pays over $40 million to associate its logo with Tiger Woods, that Reebok pays $3 mil-

I don't have to give up loving shoes.

lion to Venus Williams. (If I had known I could make that kind of money simply wearing shoes, I would have spent my whole life searching for a sponsor.) There are so many more options than even just a few years ago: leather/mesh wrestling-style bootees. Stretch-elastic fabric mules. Yoga slip-on sock boots. Not just new shapes but also new materials and methods of creating shoes. There are shoes specially engineered for running, for jumping, for standing still and schmoozing. I start scrutinizing streetwise feet and realize that while my attention was elsewhere, sneakers have morphed into cool, sleek, squish-soled sensations—they're no longer all the hideous, molded gobs of synthetic, plastic by-product they once were.

I don't have to give up loving shoes. There is hope.

Next day, I take the impossible-to-walk-in mules back to the store. I tell them that the slides did not play well with others. That they were an impulse buy. That I have since resumed my medication.

That I may have come to my senses at last.